Garden Flowers Alphabet

Coloring Book

Ruth Soffer

DOVER PUBLICATIONS
Garden City, New York

Bibliographical Note

Garden Flowers Alphabet Coloring Book is a new work, first published by Dover
Publications in 2004.

International Standard Book Number

ISBN-13: 978-0-486-43595-4
ISBN-10: 0-486-43595-4

Manufactured in the United States of America
43595411   2021
www.doverpublications.com

Publisher's Note

Here's an easy, enjoyable way for children to build alphabet, word recognition, and spelling skills, while having fun coloring. In fact, colorists of all ages can learn to recognize and identify familiar garden flowers as they bring color and hue to a bouquet of favorite blooms. Beautiful, detailed images of such eye-pleasing flora as bleeding heart, columbine, daffodils, geraniums, lilies, orchids, pansies, roses, violets, and many more invite colorists to create multi-hued floral tableaux that capture the beauty and appeal of a summer garden. Eleven color illustrations on the covers suggest coloring possibilities, but since colors often vary widely within a single species, hobbyists are free, of course, to choose their own color schemes.

A is for Azalea
(*Rhododendron nudiflorum*)

B is for Bleeding Heart
(*Dicentra spectabilis*)

C is for Columbine
(*Aquilegia canadensis*)

D is for Daffodil

(*Narcissus*)

E is for Echinacea
(*Echinacea purpurea*)

F is for Fuchsia
(*Fuchsia triphylla*)

G is for Geranium
(Pelargonium hortorum)

H is for Hibiscus
(*Hibiscus rosa-sinensis*)

I is for Iris
(*Iris germanica*)

J is for Jasmine
(Jasminum polyanthum)

K is for Kalanchoe
(*Kalanchoe blossfeldiana*)

L is for Lily
(*Lilium trigrinum*). Butterfly: Spangled Fritillary (*Speyeria cybele*).

Garden Flower Scene
(See page 32 for key to illustration)

M is for Morning Glory
(*Ipomoea learii*). Butterfly: Gorgon Copper (*Lycaena gorgon*).

N is for Nasturtium
(*Tropaeolum majus*)

O is for Orchid
(*Cymbidium*)

P is for Pansy
(Viola x wittrockiana)

21

Q is for Queen Anne's Lace
(*Daucus carota*). Butterfly: Monarch (*Danaus plexippus*).

R is for Rose
(*Rosa multiflora*)

S is for Sweet Pea
(*Lathyrus odoratus*)

T is for Trillium
(*Trillium grandiflorum*)

U is for *Uvularia perfoliata*
(Bellwort). Butterfly: Orange Sulphur (*Colias eurytheme*).

V is for Violet
(*Viola papilionacea*)

W is for Water Lily
(*Nymphaea odorata*)

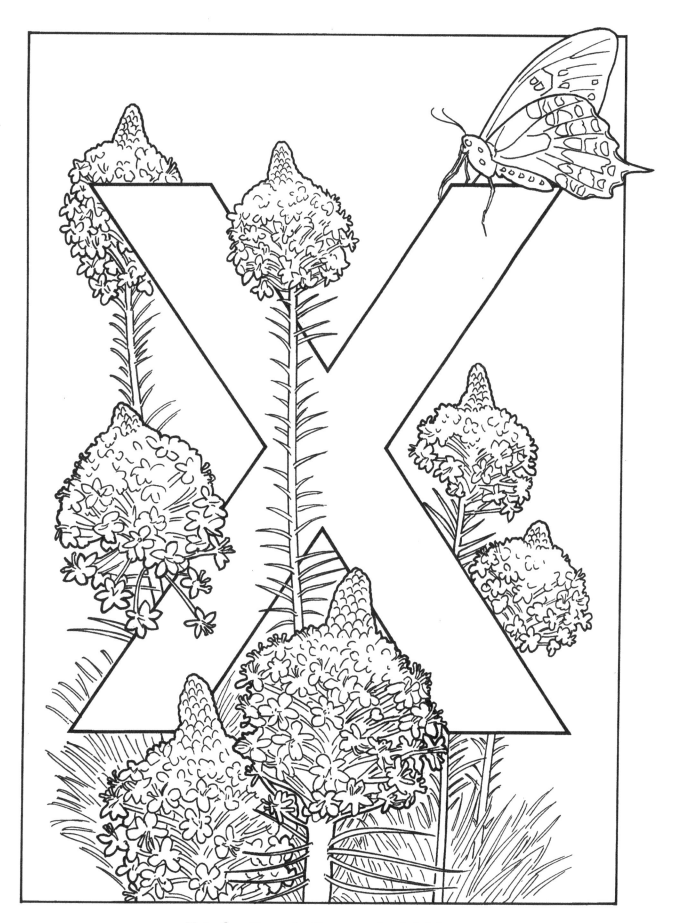

X is for *Xerophyllum asphodeloides*
(Eastern turkeybeard). Butterfly: Spicebush Swallowtail (*Papilio troilus*).

Y is for Yucca
Front: *Yucca baccata*. Background: *Yucca whipplei*.

Z is for Zinnia
(*Zinnia elegans*). Butterfly: Silver-spotted Skipper (*Epargyreus clarus*).

Key to Garden Flower Scene (pp. 16–17)

1. Sunshine (*Coreopsis basalis*)
2. Echinacea (*Echinacea purpurea*)
3. Hollyhock (*Alcea rosea*)
4. Spangled Fritillary (*Speyeria cybele*)
5. Zinnia (*Zinnia elegans*)